"I'm old, I can't take this....my heart can't take this."

These are the words that burned in my mind for 16 years.

Table of Contents

Chapter 1: Violations

It was late one night in the country; the lights were turned down, and the still of the night was setting in. As I laid there in bed with my eyes open, I heard my grandparent's voices in the next room preparing for the upcoming day and winding down for bed. Their words went silent, and the late-night talk show was the only noise until I heard another distant voice and steps nearing. The unwarranted sounds lured my grandfather out to the living room. I heard him speaking to a man with a voice I quickly recognized. It was my brother Mack.

Moments later, my bedroom door was gently opened. I turned over on my side as the light from the hallway crept in. Mack pulled the door closed behind him, and then he laid down in the bed next to me. Once he got close to me, he said, "Sharon and I had a fight. She's upset with me, so I'm spending the night here."

At the time, I was fourteen and didn't understand the significance of their fight or why he shared the story with me. Sixteen years later, I realized that I'm not the only young girl he told a story to. Over the years, Mack told many stories to many young girls that led to immoral and soul-ravishing actions. That horrific night in the country, my brother did the unthinkable and introduced me to a side of him that I didn't think was possible.

When I woke up for school the next day, I didn't recognize myself or my surroundings. I was a new me, and this was a new place. Most mornings, I was one of the first ones to the school bus, but this morning I stumbled to get ready in time. In a petrified and confused manner, I managed to make it out of the house but not before Mack ran downstairs and cut me off. He manically asked, "Did I touch you last night? Did I touch you there?" I was filled with fear, and all I could do was shrug my shoulders. He quickly and desperately began pleading, "I didn't mean it. I was drunk. Sharon and I got into a fight, and I had a lot to drink." Holding back tears, I swiftly nodded my head in hopes that he would go away and let me be. "Are you ok?" He asked. I nodded again, then he continued, "Alright, you're so cute," as he perversely pinched my cheek with his right hand before I left.

Chapter 2: Unprotected

When I arrived at school, bustling with middle school-aged children, I felt as though I was on a deserted island. It's heartbreaking how you could be around so many people and feel alone. I found my way to the cafeteria, tucked myself away, and hoped not to see the one person I didn't want to face.

That hope was short-lived. Jackson approached and sat next to me in that cafeteria, with a smile on his face as usual. I remained silent. He asked if there was something wrong. I looked over at him slowly, stared into his eyes, and responded, "no." He smiled at me, and I cried inside.

It was the last time I looked at Jackson for a long while. I could no longer see him through my new set of eyes. I grew more distant as the days, weeks, months, and years progressed. As young and vulnerable as we were, I assumed that Jackson should have known something was wrong that day and protected me. I was sadly mistaken and shouldn't have expected him to read my mind or know what I experienced.

Sixteen years later, I realized that my protectors were right in the home with me, in the next room over just an earshot away while I was violated by one of the closest members in the family tree. The rest of my school day after the tragic experience was a blur. Before I knew it, I was back in the country, walking up the long road to the old house. As I neared, I could see my grandmother sitting near a burning trash pile 15 feet away from the old house. I walked up to her and said, "Umm, Nanny." She silently turned and looked at me, and I continued, "Umm, I need to talk to you about something."

She turned away from me and redirected her attention to the trash pile. My feelings crumbled while she poked around the pile with a stick. The look on her face was as if I was getting ready to burden her with the weight of the world. I didn't let it stop me. After adjusting her clothing, she said, "ok," signifying me to say what I disturbed her for. I blurted out, "Mack touched me!"

She didn't respond or acknowledge me. I continued, "He touched me in a way that a brother shouldn't touch a sister." She turned halfway towards me and nonchalantly said, "Well, did he say anything to you?" As I stared at her, confused and frightened, my heart pounded, and I wondered if I did the right thing.

I managed to say, "Yes, mam. He said that he and Sharon had a fight and that he was drunk." As my grandmother adjusted her focus back toward the trash pile, she responded, "Well, if he said that he was drunk, then he was drunk." An awkward silence arrived, then she emphasized, "Don't tell your grandfather."

As I breathed the country air and the smell of burning trash infiltrated the air, I sunk to another unfamiliar place. Everything around me that I had known to be true was now a lie. I looked across the yard, and I saw my grandfather in the distance. He'd just finished a project of some handy work. As he approached us at the pile, he asked, "What's going on?"

My grandmother quickly replied, "Nothing, she's getting ready to go put her things up from school." As devastation crept in, I glanced at my grandfather and quickly departed. Later that night, I could still hear my grandmother's voice in my ears, "Don't tell your grandfather." It replayed repeatedly, and it was the worst voice that any child could hear.

As the next day came and went, I could no longer hold my silence. I got off of the school bus and headed up the long road to the old house. I saw my grandfather in the distance, clearing the land from the shrubbery. I went into the house, threw my backpack on the bed, kicked my shoes off, and watched him from a window as he maneuvered his way through the thick of the land. I followed him through the house, window to window, and door to door. He finally made his way to the side entrance of the old house, where I intercepted him. After we casually greeted each other, he said, "Your grandma ought to be home soon." My eyes widened, and my breathing increased as my heart started beating rapidly. He had no idea, but this was my red flag that I had to ring the alarm, and I didn't have a tremendous amount of time to do it. After a period of extended silence, I said, "Granddaddy, there's something I need to tell you." He looked at me concerned and said, "ok."

As he took a seat across from me in the living room, I had his undivided attention. I knew at that moment that I had someone who would protect me. I explained what happened two nights ago and told him that my grandmother instructed me not to tell him. I intently studied his facial expression while I was telling him what happened. Shock, sadness, hurt, confusion, and anger boiled over. He became enraged, and his fire excited me. His reaction provoked the moment when it felt like I was the closest to having a father. He reacted just like I imagined a father would. He was going to protect me, no matter what.

Moments later, my grandmother pulled up in the yard. I could hear the engine of the old truck as she parked along the house's side entrance. Consequently, my grandfather had disappeared. My grandmother made her way to the side entrance door and pulled the sliding door back as she entered the living room in the old house while I watched from a chair nearby. By this time, my grandfather reappeared. I saw my grandmother's face go stale when she looked up at him.

He charged towards her with a twelve-gauge rifle in his right hand, swiftly swinging back and forth. As he got closer, she yelled out, "Henry! What's wrong?" He snatched the keys from her hand as he walked past her with no response. She swung around in disbelief again. "Henry, what is going on?!" She yelled. While getting into the truck, my grandfather aggressively responded, "You know what's wrong, Jean? She told me!" The heavy truck door creaked as he slammed it shut and then started the engine. My grandmother pleaded, "Henry, please, don't do this!" Then began weeping as he backed the truck up, swung it around, and sped off, leaving a golden smoke cloud of dust from the old country road. I quickly went into my room and shut the door. I was afraid of what may happen, what I may have caused. I was fearful that my granddaddy would be sent away.

Three hours later, as I sat near my bedroom window staring out of the tiny rectangular holes in the screen and inhaling the smell of the country air, I could hear the engine to the old truck in the distance. My grandfather had returned. I ran to the front porch. A part of me was running to make sure that he had not been hurt as well.

I was also running because I wanted to know what occurred between him and Mack and if Mack had admitted his wrongdoing. I was curious if my grandfather believed me and if he was still going to protect me. I feared getting hurt again. These thoughts rapidly ran through my mind as I stared with big eyes at him walking up to the old house. His body slouched, head hung, and a rifle pointed to the ground in his limp right hand. When he arrived at the steps where I was curiously waiting, he looked at my face with saddened eyes and said, "I'm sorry gal." Then he walked past me and into the old house. I swung around and just stood still. I wanted to know what happened, but I knew my place as a child, so I waited.

I heard my grandparents talking in the living room. I remained on the front porch steps with my face in my hands. I stared into the country yard and listened to the late spring day as the sunset and crickets, grasshoppers, woodpeckers, dragonflies, and all of nature's sounds filled my ears.

The next day I wondered if I should tell one of my trusted teachers, but I didn't understand the world they lived in. Because I didn't have anything in common with them, and we were different races, I assumed and feared there would be a lack of sensitivity. I worried about the potential repercussions if they handled it wrong. Will I be beaten if the school counselor phones home and asks questions? Will the police be called? Worst of all, would I end up back in a foster home separated from what I knew as home for the past six years? The thought of going back into the system as a foster child frightened me. I feared that I would once again be separated from my sister, the one being that I knew who loved me and could protect me without a doubt.

I didn't share my incident with my teachers, Jackson, or anyone. However, I could no longer wait for my grandfather to tell me what happened when he stormed off that day with his rifle. After my long walk up the road to the old house the next day, I found him watching television in the den. I walked up to him and bluntly asked, "So what happened, granddaddy? Did you talk to him?"

He turned and looked at me, then said, "Yeah, I talked with Mack." "And?" I quickly asked him. I grew a bit anxious and irritated at the fact I had to provoke this conversation. My grandfather responded, "He said he didn't do anything wrong." I felt the heat brewing under my dark cheeks as I glared at him in disappointment. He slightly raised his voice and asked, "What do you want me to do?" I immediately yelled, "I want you to tell him that he can no longer come here and that you will not allow him to hurt me again!" He looked the other way and responded, "I can't do that, gal. He's my child too. He's my son! You want me to tell my own son that he can't come here anymore?" "YES!!" I yelled back.

He sat there staring at me as I ran away in the opposite direction. I flung my bedroom door open, slammed it behind me, and threw myself on the bed face down to muffle the cries as my heart broke into a million pieces. The summer was quickly approaching, and the more time I spent in the old house, the more I worried about the predator returning. I knew I had to make a quick move.

Chapter 3: Domino Effect

I began packing bags of clothing, shoes, and a grocery bag full of personal hygiene items. I threw away all things that left any traces of me in that old house. The following day when I knew my grandparents would be away, I called my sister, Evelyn. Evelyn and I had been through so much together in our younger years. Even though she was just five years and four months older than me, I knew that she would protect me by any means. I felt her protection through the years without even really knowing what that protection was.

Twenty years later, I remember the phone call as if it just happened. "Evelyn," I stammered. "I need to talk to you." "Oh Lord," she replied, already grasping the reason for my call before I could even verbalize the nature of my new reality. She took a long sigh and then rocked my core by saying, "I knew this day would come." Shocked, I managed to ask, "Which day?" She encouraged me to tell her what happened, then I cleared my throat and said, "Well, Mack touched me in a way that he shouldn't have. I told Nanny, and she said not to worry about it because he was drunk." After I finished venting, I asked Evelyn to please come get me.

About an hour and a half later, a burgundy delta 88 pulled up. It was Evelyn. She came to rescue me. I remember the feeling of freedom and peace I felt the entire ride into the city. I was with family now. Someone who loved me and appreciated my life. We sat down alone that evening, and Evelyn told me a story about the years of abuse that she suffered at Mack's hands. I wept inside and was in a state of shock as I listened to her speak.

Currently, I still find myself grieving at times for her loss of innocence at the hands of an absolute monster. Being the young and mature mother that she was, Evelyn had me help her arrange a picnic the next day with her friend, kids, and I, at a park near downtown. It was a joyous time, one of my happiest memories ever.

I remained with her and my niece and nephew over the next year. We had our minor disagreements as sisterhood has, but our love remained solid. When I first transitioned into my new life, I grew closer with my other sister Christine. She also confessed to us that she'd been a victim of Mack as well. She tearfully told us that she was only eight years old when he committed his first sexual act against her and that it continued into her young adult years. His torment had become a regularity. We cried together.

It wasn't long after I blew the whistle that word began to spread like wildfire throughout the very small city near the old country town. My voice began to have a domino effect. Women and girls of all ages, races, and backgrounds began reaching out to my sisters and me. People of the general public who knew our family or in some fashions were family. Two women that Mack impregnated came forward and confessed that they were taken advantage of. I vividly remember one of them describing how she was just 14 and Mack was 18. He started seeing her whenever he could and continuously avoided her mother. She admitted that she was struck by all the hype that surrounded Mack. A varsity football player and star athlete with what seemed to be a promising future, as colleges from all over were scouting him. He had a flashy sports car during a time when most teenagers did not even have a driver's license.

She was honest, and we understood how she must've felt. She told us about a time he ripped her panties off underneath the bleachers after a high school football game and forced himself on her against her wishes. Nine months later, she gave birth to a sweet baby boy. She shared with us how our grandparents took her in during her pregnancy and treated her like royalty due to her mother threatening to call the police.

Chapter 4: (Cover-Ups)

Not too long after that occurrence, the second mother reached out to Evelyn in empathy to tell her how sorry she was about everything. "I should've protected y'all," she cried to Evelyn. Then she shared the most vulgar and explicit acts that she was subjected to by Mack. She was only at the tender age of 15 when our grandparents allowed Mack to bring her into their suburban home as a "live in" girlfriend.

Mack was ten years her senior. He beat her when she wouldn't do what he wanted, and often those beatings would end in a vicious sexual act. I remember seeing him choke her at the foot of the stairs once when I was four years old. My grandmother stood in the nearby kitchen and calmly said, "Ok, that's enough, Mack, stop." The young lady cried her heart out while her fair skin was marked with profound wounds.

A lot of things went on in that house. I recall walking into an upstairs bedroom once and the eerie feeling that I got when I saw what had to be hundreds of long green welts stained into the stark white walls. My grandmother had given a brutal beating to a female cousin of mine. Years later, this same cousin confessed that she had been beaten because she outed Mack for attacking her.

Of all the cover-ups throughout the years, I can't help but wonder about all the acts and violations they would never have to cover up because only Mack, his victims, and the good Lord Himself knew about them. The stories continued to unfold. I encountered years of stories, mostly from women who confessed that they were victims of his as well. By the summer of 2000, nearly 20 different women had spoken out about being raped, molested, or experienced some sort of unwanted sexual act by Mack. One woman described to a close family friend how she was literally chased down by Mack and brutally raped right on her parent's lawn one night. He was an absolute monster.

One thing that all the stories had in common was how each woman felt that his status protected him and ultimately would result in their reporting being dismissed or even frowned upon. It's beyond me how so many women could feel like holding someone accountable for violating them would consequently ruin their own lives.

A predator almost always knows the weakest and most vulnerable of their victims. They purposely prey upon those they feel they can forever silence. This is what I came to learn about Mack. They often don't realize that their obsession and very being is a sickness that can transform them into a complete savage that is incoherent to everything normal and logical. When the mind is impaired, it is at risk of missing even the most obvious signs of danger. This danger that I speak of regarding Mack was me. His sickness was too strong to think of the possible outcome that would follow him sneaking into my bed that night in the old country house. It was too blind to see the fighter in me, even at 14. Too arrogant to sense the intelligence and maturity in me. Too hungry to care and too evil to sense my strong spirit of discernment and pure innocence.

Twenty years is a long time to recover and pick up the pieces. Even still, I have some hard days when I think about my lineage and how so many things and so much heartbreak could've been prevented if someone had just decided to do the right thing.

Chapter 5: Enabler

Enabler

en·a·bler

/iˈnāblər,eˈnāblər/

noun

1. A person or thing that makes something possible.

In my 34 years of life, I have never looked up the definition of enabler. On August 22, 2019, I felt compelled to research the exact definition. The word in the definition that stands out to me immediately is "thing." For years, generations of women in my family have tried figuring out what, how, and why my grandmother allowed these terrible things to happen.

Is she human? Does she have a heart? Is she a thing? This was basically what we tried to figure out. Years of discord and grief in one family are a difficult thing to repair. However, I imagined more effort. Not only did she not try, but she wouldn't acknowledge any of it as well. My mother shouted her childhood story from the rooftops, even detailing the acts of her offender. Consequently, my grandmother threatened to kill her if she ever voiced it again.

Surprisingly, her offender, along with her two younger sisters, was my grandfather. Unfortunately, the only grandfather we knew. As the years passed, I recalled my mother having emotional outbursts regarding the years of abuse she suffered at her step-father's hands. He began touching her and her sisters at a very young age, and by the time she was 12, he eventually started raping her, and it went on for the next three years. At age 15, my mother gave birth to her firstborn, Mack. Not long after his birth, she traveled down a vicious path of doing drugs, stealing, and running with local thugs. This cycle continued for nearly 50 years. She missed a half-century of memories, including childbirths, graduations, marriages, military deployments, and deaths.

One of my most challenging times was my high school graduation. The absence of my mother and the overwhelming feelings I had that night in the arena caused the detriment. Out of my accomplishments, this one stood out the most, and I remembered it as if it was yesterday. I had taken such ownership of my life at this time. I was one year into my journey with the US Army. I was able to financially cover all the festivities and perks that came with being a senior in high school, and it was a great feeling.

The arena was packed. Reluctantly, I moved back into the old house in the country with my grandparents due to a minor dispute between Evelyn and I that occurred one year after I had moved to the city with her. I didn't have a fancy new outfit, and I did my own hair for graduation, but it was a great feeling there in the arena, nonetheless. My great Cousin Vee and her family were there to show their support along with my grandparents. I didn't think I was a popular child, but the stadium roared as I floated on air to receive my diploma. I can't even describe how freeing that moment was. It was like my light to my new beginning.

Chapter 6: Things Left Unsaid

As I walked down the steps of the stage and then down the long aisle to return to my seat, I saw Jackson stand up and step into the aisle with an ever so serious look in his eyes. I had not spoken to him since the day I left him sitting in the middle school cafeteria. I was extremely withdrawn as we went into our freshman year, then moved to the city the summer before my sophomore year. Once I returned my junior year, I readjusted to the change and signed on with the army that summer. Returning from boot camp the summer before my senior year was an absolute drag in my mind. My brain and body had been completely transformed. I was no longer in the mind frame of a high school senior. I was a full-grown adult with a level of discipline that would travel with me for the rest of my life, and I had little to no tolerance for stupidity. I was almost too mature, honestly. The immaturity of my classmates and peers annoyed me. I withdrew from sports and most extracurricular activities. I just wanted to get out of there and start my new life as an adult. Needless to say, I was so overwhelmed with graduation, but freedom wouldn't be the only reason for these feelings.

As I neared the end of the aisle where Jackson was standing, he held out his arms and hugged me tightly. I wish I would have never let go. It was his way of saying, "For whatever reason, we never reconnected. It's ok, and I never stopped loving you." I was very emotional as I pulled away from him, and he said, "Don't cry now." I quickly asked him if he was going to the lock-in at the school afterward, and he said, "Yes, I'll see you there."

I must have turned around to look at the entry door at least 30 times that night, yet no Jackson. The next morning, I woke up to the news that he died in a car accident along with his nephew. Eighteen years later, I still bury my face in the palms of my hands and scream bloody murder over the heartbreak and shock I felt after his death. All those years, all the silence, and then he was gone.

My mother has endured enough losses for several lifetimes. She would periodically reappear after years in prison, but her releases were typically short-lived. With little to no genuine family support and negative bystanders who awaited her return to prison and gossiped about her demise, my mother relapsed repetitively. Eventually, she completed nursing school and seemed to be on a healthy and hopeful track, but her past demons would not let her prevail. I imagined that she was defeated in her own right. Even earning the initials of LVN behind her name was not enough to wash away the years of trauma and violation she had been exposed to by an enabler whom she called mother.

Her prison sentences became longer and longer, each time more grueling than the last. Three years, five years, eight, and then eventually a couple of ten-year sentences, which were the most devastating. My mother had five children, and each time she went away, she took a little piece of mine and Evelyn's heart and soul. She left behind one incarcerated for his own crimes. The other two were coming into their adulthood with little time for anyone but themselves and the lives they were trying to make. The youngest two, Evelyn and I, were tossed into the system and in the care of foster guardians.

Chapter 7: Foster Care

I remember my foster parent vividly. She was a tall statuesque woman with a short haircut, wide face, hearty voice, and infectious smile that donned a front tooth outlined in gold plating. I don't know if I loved this lady or if she loved me but what I did know is that she provided me a home and shelter that wasn't always filled with great days, but there were more good days than bad. It was a safe haven for me with the structure that I had never had. She rewarded us for things like good grades and hauled those of us with straight-A report cards down to the local Toys "R" Us to pick up a toy of our choice or often of hers. Play-dough was always a popular choice with her. I know her pockets weren't deep, but her expression of love was. She wasn't perfect, but I admired her for trying.

I slept in a room with at least 4 to 5 other girls. The younger of us bunking two by two in bunk beds, and the older tribe settled in a full-size bed nearby. Shortly after placement in the house, my sister and I were separated. I found out years later that she was transferred to a teenage girl's home somewhere in the city. I missed her dearly and wept for some time after her departure. I was swift and picked up on the fact that my new guardian was agitated by whining, which resulted in punishment. For this reason, I learned not to remain in my feelings and fall into a routine. She'd yell for us on a Sunday evening to bring the "barrette box," which was full of "bobos" or "knockers" and hair ornaments of all sorts. There was usually a small, handled bristle brush, rat-tail comb, and blue magic hair grease in the box. She meticulously took her time to take care of each one of our hair for school the next day and finished her work by slathering her heavy, greased hands over our little cheeks for moisturizing. It was the simple things such as mass hairstyling that made the brick three-bedroom house a home. She kept a close watch and ensured that we completed homework assignments, carefully checking over them as we sat at the kitchen table for whatever meal she'd prepared for us in the evenings. She was a little intimidating, but she was all I knew. I still couldn't understand for the life of me why she had sent my sister away. I believed wholeheartedly that if I made enough straight-A report cards and managed not to agitate her pet peeves, she would let my sister return.

I believe I became one of her preferred children seeing that my foster siblings would get frequent and alarming punishments, including being sometimes dragged through the home by their ponytails. No matter how many A's I made and how much I managed to remain on her good side, nothing seemed to be working on getting my sister back. I remember even being bold enough to ask if she could return when I felt that I had done my due diligence, but the answer was never a yes. I was young and not sure how much time had passed being in the home. I assume that it was a year or less. Eventually, my time there would come to an abrupt halt.

My foster guardian received a call one day, and she kept me from taking the school bus that morning with my foster siblings. She was filled with what I believe was a touch of melancholy and a façade of pretending to be tough and unmoved, but I saw it in her eyes and felt it in her heart when she hugged me goodbye that she was saddened to see me go. On the other hand, I was nothing short of elated! All I could think about was being with my sister again.

That thought delighted me. After settling down from the news, my foster guardian did my hair as usual. This time she took particular care to detail, creating three perfectly parted ponytails with bobo's barrettes and bows. She dressed me in what was usually a "Sunday dress" (red and green plaid), nice-ruffled socks with patent leather slippers, and then moisturized my small face with the blue magic residue left on her large, warm hands. I smiled up at her, and she knew I was excited about the whole ordeal, but she showed no signs of excitement.

Two hours later, I was off. I don't remember what the social worker looked like that drove me to the meeting, but I do remember pulling up to a humongous building after what seemed like the longest drive ever. The building was red brick and had the letters "LP" on the corner of it. I recall a ride up an elevator and the doors opening to a sitting area, and then I was escorted into a room where an older woman and man were sitting.

The woman wore a shiny pink dress, short and curly red hair, red lipstick, and had squinty eyes. She smiled at me. It was my grandparents. It took me a while to adjust, and now I know the purpose of the meeting room was meant just for that reason, a transition space. Shortly after arriving, my sister came into the room, and all was right in the world as far as I was concerned.

Chapter 8: Generational Curses

We happily departed from the large building with our grandparents to the old house in the country. The first night was immaculate. There was a slender console table behind the couch in the living area and a pretty crystal bell on it that I was intrigued to ring but convinced myself not to. We made a stop to see another family member on our way to the old house. We traveled down a windy road in the old truck, swaying back and forth with every bump. Soon we came to a small wooden home where a cheerful little boy broke through the screen door and made a run for it towards the old truck. He was about my age and recognized my sister and I immediately.

It was my dear nephew who, over the years, became more like a brother to me. He was beaming with excitement. His fat little round cheeks shined under the moonlight. These were some of the best memories of the life change for my sister and me, but like most things, the joyous feelings quickly faded away.

The next several weeks were some of the hardest ever. I ended up getting my very first lashing over a white lie that any young child would tell out of fear. It was a most traumatizing experience as I was stripped down to my panties in front of my grandfather and nephew, who was just five months younger than I. My grandmother must have struck me with the leather belt over 20 times. When I tried to escape, my grandfather pinned me between his bony knees and restricted my arms. It had to be the most embarrassing experience ever. It wasn't the discipline. It was my body being exposed. I had never experienced anything like this before. Even at that young tender age, it felt wrong, and I knew I was being violated.

Less than 48 hours later, I was physically disciplined with an extension cord for not cleaning the house properly. I had completely transformed mentally and began to realize that this was now my new life. I remember wanting to call my foster mother to tell her what happened, but I feared the potential consequences if I told her what was happening in the home. I became withdrawn, walked on eggshells, and was terrified that I would be beaten for anything that I did. I remember being afraid to even leave food on my plate during dinner. I would sit for an extended period of time if I had a spoonful of peas or a piece of chicken that wasn't clean to the bone.

On the other hand, my sister seemed to be settling in, but this would eventually only be the naïve thoughts of an eight-year-old child. Though my sister wasn't physically beaten as often, she was suffering through something far worse. She was a star athlete, made good grades, and absolutely gorgeous. She had a smile that could light up a room and a captivating personality. Though my eight-year-old eyes saw all that glittered, Evelyn was not happy nor ok.

No matter how great she was in sports or how gorgeous she was, it didn't change the fact that she was sexually abused consistently. Once Mack got word about us being in our grandparents' custody, it wasn't long before he came lingering around. Oftentimes his visits were brief, but upon his departure, he would cleverly give my grandparents a reason on why he needed to take Evelyn with him.

How could I be in this home with my sister and be so oblivious to what was happening right in front of my face? But even worse, how could my grandparents not see? Or did they see? They had to know! In the disguise of a brother, this predator went from taking her away on the weekends to coming to take her in the middle of the week. How was this happening? He would give bogus reasons for taking her like, "Oh, I want to buy her some new shoes or new clothes." My sister would return not only empty-handed but abused, broken, and teary-eyed. Was it so hard? This is the question that I have for my grandparents today. Was it really that hard to simply take responsibility and say no!? For the life of me, I can't understand why they came to pick us up at the brick building that day. Why not leave us in the system if they were going to allow him to abuse us? Why?

These questions, along with the pain and actions that were imposed upon us in that old country house, had a stronghold on us for years and eventually began to shape the structure of our lives. We were like birds without wings. When Evelyn was 16, my grandmother found a love letter written for her by a male classmate. I was too young to fully understand or read the contents of the letter, but it was clearly a letter of affection. My grandmother completely flipped out. For some reason, Mack was there. My grandmother summoned Evelyn into the kitchen and questioned her about the letter and then began grabbing anything within her reach and flinging it at my sister with all her might. She threw the iron, ironing board, broomstick, a chair, and a 2 x 4 wood plank. That woman hit my 16-year-old frail sister over her back with a 2 x 4 plank. That had to be the last straw for Evelyn. Things just continued going downhill from there, and in an instant, she was gone.

Once again, I was without my sister. I remember feeling so lost and abused. Over the next couple of years, Evelyn ended up moving in with an older cousin, friends, and eventually into her boyfriend's parents' house. She was 18 and pregnant with her first child. My niece was a new lifeline for Evelyn and a true blessing from the Lord above. One may wonder how being eighteen and pregnant is a blessing, but that child, along with those that followed, were blessings, nonetheless. My sister attempted suicide several times in the old house. The last two times were nearly fatal. Present-day, Evelyn is a mother to five and grandmother to two and counting. God is so good. Christine gave birth to nine children and is a grandmother as well. Christine didn't talk very much about her abuse. She only disclosed that it started at about the age of 8 and how vulgar it was. Throughout the years, I often thought about how different our lives would've been if we weren't abused. It has been a plaguing generational curse in my family.

Christine is doing well after becoming a breast cancer survivor in 2017. We have a brother a few years younger than Mack, who seems to be making it. I am blessed because each of my siblings, including Mack, are living and breathing, but at times, I felt broken due to life's trials and tribulations that have kept us estranged.

The absence of our mother has taken a harsh toll. Fifty years of absence that we can no longer get back was squandered. Life is hard, but God is able. Though we have been a family apart for decades, the good Lord has truly kept us all. Even though we don't get together often, there is some form of love when we do. Currently, I have a total of 26 nieces and nephews, and the great-nieces and nephews are rolling in as well. I have struggled over the years for not having a relationship with all of them due to the estranged relationships with my siblings, but in time my Lord and Savior has healed those wounds and feelings of guilt. I can't recall a time that I've ever been in any of their presence and didn't feel love.

My mother has been on free land since December 2015. I was married and working on the southside of Houston. Evelyn picked her up from the bus station upon her release. She was always the closest to our mother. I had a mixture of emotions at the time, and I imagine we all did. There had been so many years of her going in and out of prison. We never really knew how long it would be before she went back and honestly if she'd ever be home for good.

Current day, she is still going strong. She has her own place and a job that treats her well. She's recently been diagnosed with cancer, but again, God is able. At the age of 71, it seems as though she's decided to continue living life on her own terms. We aren't the Brady Bunch by any means, but I can proudly say that she is able to speak with all five of her children on a consistent basis. I have concluded that we all come into this world by God's sufficient grace, and we will leave by his everlasting mercy. We cannot choose the life that we're given or the cards we're dealt. However, we can create the life that we were born to live. My mother has shared a lot with me, and every time we have a deep conversation I learn something new.

One time she shared a story about one of the many times she told my grandmother about her step-father raping her and her sisters. She said, "We were living in West Covina, California, and I told Nanny that I didn't understand why she didn't believe me. I turned to Teresa (my mother's middle sister) and said, "Tell her, Teresa! Tell her what he did to you. Tell her that he raped you too." Teresa denied it ever happened. I slapped your aunt in the face, and your grandmother broke a chair over my back and beat me down."

I could hear the hurt in her voice as she went on to say, "All I ever wanted was for her to acknowledge that she believed me." Listening to my mother's childhood stories was saddening but still didn't seem to cause me to have any ill will towards my grandmother. I was ten years old when she first told me about the abuse. I didn't hold it against my grandmother or my grandfather, even for that matter. However, I admit I was careful when it came to my grandfather. I stopped feeling free around him. Very distinctly, I remember when my small chest started forming at the age of 10. Although I hadn't learned much about my body, I had the common sense to know that it was time for me to be in an undergarment. I was careful not to draw any unwanted attention. For this intuition at such a young age, I was grateful. It was the same intuition that helped me escape from the old country house that summer and the same intuition that has been inside of me since I was four years old and hiding behind a brick column from a Caucasian man in his 30s who tried kidnapping me by luring me in with candy.

For as long as I can remember, my sisters and I were surrounded by predators of all shapes, sizes, races, and genders. Over the years, Evelyn has shared her personal stories with me, detailing the trauma she experienced from one of our mother's boyfriends at the age of six. From the age of 12, she experienced abuse from the hands of Christine's then-husband. It was sickening finding out how she used to shield me from becoming a victim during certain encounters with random people who were allowed to be around us by wrapping herself around me tightly as she was being fondled. The amount of unconditional love, self-sacrifice, and courage that this must have taken was unfathomable for me, even in my mid-30s. I can't imagine how she endured such horrible things at such a young age. I've always looked up to her for her strength, strong work ethic, and resilience. There have been many days when I think about all the great things she could've done had she not been subjected to the things she went through as a child and young adult. Currently, she is a whole and beautiful young lady, but I wonder what her future may have been if her upbringing wasn't so horrific.

Christine has never been as open as Evelyn and me about the abuse we endured, but I believe it was because she had her wings broken very early in life and that things were a lot more severe than what she said they were. In fact, this is one of her sweetest (unhealthy) but sweetest qualities. Despite some of the awful things she shared with us, she has mostly been a lighthearted and spirited being. She, too, is doing ok, but I also think about the possibilities and "what ifs" for her life as well.

My mother went through and endured despite it all. Pulling herself up or at least trying to the best way she knew how and even putting herself through nursing school. Though we are all capable of anything through the grace of God, this had to be a definite challenge given her circumstances. Especially after going through childhood trauma, years of drug abuse, and lengthy prison stays. She was a strong and intelligent woman that should have had a promising future but simply could not escape the demons of her past. I've often wondered how life for her and her children would have been if things were different in her life. I wonder now if the simple acknowledgment from my grandmother could not necessarily reverse what happened. Clearly, that is far from possible, but at least the thought somewhat triggers the road to healing. Maybe simply acknowledging her pain and trauma would have led her down a different path rather than a vicious cycle of criminal activity. I wonder if my grandmother has given that any thought. Surely, she has. How could she not? How in 50 years could she not? Would it have been so hard to simply acknowledge her daughter's truth one on one? My grandmother has always been a woman of great pride for whatever reason. However, pride becomes poison when one can't do something as simple as hearing their child out and acknowledge them. Even if she didn't believe or didn't want to believe, my question to her today would be, "Was it all worth it? Was it worth

50 years of your child's life down the drain and in return not being able to mother her own kids?"

I don't solely blame my grandmother for it all, but there's no denying that she enabled her husband, which had a ripple effect with Mack and cursed her entire lineage. As I stated previously, I truly didn't hold it against either her or my grandfather, but when history repeated itself with Mack, the same enabling spirit raised its ugly head. It was another chance to do the right thing, even if it wasn't the easy thing, but she still turned the other cheek. This time it was personal. In my opinion, it was cold, careless, and calculated. Her defense would be, "I'm old. I can't take this. My heart can't take this. If you go in there (local CPS office) and tell them people that something happened to you, I will have a heart attack." What in hell makes a grandmother say this to her 14-year-old molested grandchild? This is my truth, and it has affected me well into my adulthood. I always knew it was the reason I had not established any successful relationships. I hadn't been able to heal yet. Even when I knew certain individuals that I was involved with had nothing but genuine love for me. I found ways not to make it work. I have had some decent people in my life that I could've possibly had a future with, but relationships got squandered because of my painful past.

Chapter 9: New Beginnings

At the age of 33, I had been married and divorced. Before my marriage, I'd been engaged and proposed to a number of times. I'm clearly wife material, but I read recently that when we are hurt and unhealed with things that negatively festered over the years, we self-consciously believe that we don't deserve love. I know this now, but I didn't know it over the years. I've been through a series of failed relationships. Some of them were necessary to break off, some should have never been, and some that were a direct result of my past trauma. For years, I have had a tough time with intimacy with a man. Before my assault, I experienced adolescent kissing and being held by Jackson, but after the assault, I was very withdrawn, and any attempt at intimacy felt like an attack. No matter how much I cared for the person I was with. Regardless of how much they cared for me, and despite it being consensual, it still felt like I was being attacked. There have been times when I felt like I couldn't breathe by just having someone lay on top of me. My marriage suffered in this area. Being married to someone who had experienced their own sexual dysfunction as a child certainly didn't add a plus to the equation. I have learned that sexual abuse/exposure at a young age has a number of different effects on people. I saw for some it caused promiscuity, perversion, or hyper-sexual behaviors. Withdrawal and dysfunction are my after-effects. Life is hard, but God is able.

In 2017, exactly two years after I married my husband, I found a friend and confidant in a female I began a friendship with while going through my divorce. For the most part, I've always been an honest person. When I made a mental connection with this new friend, I immediately went home and told my husband. I mentioned her interest to him months prior and that I didn't quite know what to make of it, but he just brushed it off and said, "Oh, she's probably just being nice." Once I brought it to his attention again and that I had mutual feelings, he took it more seriously. As things were already strained in our relationship, we decided to finalize the divorce, and I became extremely distant. Shortly after, I moved out of the house and into a one-bedroom apartment that

I secured soon after we decided on the divorce. I couldn't live under the same roof a minute more. It was misery. I was locking myself in the master bedroom at night and finding something to do during the day, so we did not encounter each other. He slept down the hall in the guest room and pleaded with me to give the marriage a chance, but I felt in my heart that his motivation was mainly because I had emotionally moved on. I believe that he loved me, but it wasn't enough. There was so much damage between us from verbal abuse, mainly due to what I considered infidelity and just an overall dysfunction prior to dating. I loved him, but I was no longer in love. He was a good friend when I needed one, but it probably should've never gone any further than just friendship, to be honest. I don't have any regrets, but this is my truth.

About four months after moving into my apartment, I received a phone call from the female friend one night. She was clearly in distress. She told me that she had been physically attacked by her live-in partner and asked if she could spend the night on my couch. I welcomed her with open arms. What was initially meant to be a night or two turned into a 2 ½ year relationship. We were inseparable. She was the peanut butter to my jelly. It was easy with us and light. It was everything that I thought I needed. Although things were effortless and good with us, I still felt that I owed myself some time and solitude after my divorce. I stayed and hoped that she would get her own space. I knew I needed the space, but she counted on me. Rather than risk losing her, I caved in. Two and a ½ years later, I firmly decided to get the solitude that I still felt that I needed more than ever. Things were not as light and carefree as they once were. Although I felt love, I observed some things that were highly unhealthy and once again dysfunctional. My health took a turn for the worse, and I became unhappy once again. I needed alone time, time with God, and no distractions.

So, here I am, navigating my way through life and my following chapters to come. When you are a victim of sexual abuse, you gain what I refer to as a sixth sense. After my attack, I could sense when I was in the presence of a monster. It's not always obvious at first sight, but eventually, after only a minute or so, the fine hairs on the back of my neck would stand. I'll never forget being about four years old, living with a family friend, and playing in a neighborhood yard in the small town. There was a home on the corner which had a large brick wall at the edge of the yard, which was a subdivision entrance sign. An old dirty white van with no windows crept around the corner and slowed when the driver noticed me. He was a Caucasian man that appeared in his 30s, had sandy blonde hair, blue eyes, and a sun-kissed face. He smiled, and I scooted closer to the brick wall, almost hiding myself. Then he leaned out of the window of the van and motioned for me to come here with his index finger moving swiftly in a flickering motion. This terrified me, so I completely hid behind the brick wall while my little heart pounded. In my young mind, I figured if he couldn't see me, then I would be safe. My Lord and Savior certainly tucked me in His wings because a minute later, the van slowly crept down the road in the opposite direction. This type of thing was common back then, but I can't help but ask myself why?

The creeps didn't stop with him. They were all around all the time. The monsters came in all different shapes, sizes, races, and genders. I firmly believe that predators know the weak and can sniff out who their victims will be. Evelyn sadly had a mark on her. She endured pain and suffering from strangers, the mates of family members, male and female, and family as well. Evelyn and I both have experienced sexual propositions or attempted attacks from close cousins. There always seemed to be an unspoken past occurrence of events with the younger generation. Some female cousins spoke about the male cousins' private parts, flagrant gestures, or actions between cousins and siblings. You name it, and our family had it. We encountered male family members who almost seemed to have a sense of entitlement to certain females in our family. It wasn't rocket science to figure out that there had likely been relations between some of our family members. It wouldn't surprise me if some relations still exist.

Current day for me is exceptional and I feel complete. My spiritual walk is nowhere near perfect, but I know that I have a unique and special relationship with the Lord. He has kept me and continues to keep me every day. I feel so blessed in this particular moment because I know what the Lord has for me is for me. I aspire to meet with girls and women worldwide, who experienced struggles similar to mine. It's nearly surreal that I can feel these things already happening. To a degree, I have always seen my highest self, even in my less confident times. My mother is in recovery from her battle with cancer. She is living the best life she can. I've often told her the rest of her life should be the best of her life. My happiness may not be the same as her happiness, so I've learned to cope the best I can. My sister, Evelyn, is living and mainly for her children and now grandchildren. I'm so excited to see what the Lord has in store for her. My other three siblings are in their worlds. May God always have His hand on them.

My main motivation for writing this book was to finally get therapeutic healing and help others. I pray that if a young girl is experiencing things like me, she can find hope in these words and pages, the strength and courage to push forward, speak out, and get help. I am more than grateful to share my story with the world.

Printed in Great Britain
by Amazon

56711268R00036